Life Cycles

Bean

Louise Spilsbury

Heinemann Library
Chicago, Illinois

Customer Service   888-454-2279

Visit our website at www.heinemannlibrary.com

Photo research by Maria Joannou and Debra Weatherley
Designed by Michelle Lisseter
Printed and bound in China by South China Printing Company

09 08 07 06 05
10 9 8 7 6 5 4 3 2 1

Library of Congress Cataloging-in-Publication Data
Spilsbury, Louise.
   Bean / Louise Spilsbury.
       p. cm. -- (Life cycles)
   Includes index.
   ISBN 1-4034-6769-2 (hardcover) -- ISBN 1-4034-6774-9 (pbk.)
   1. Beans--Life cycles--Juvenile literature. I. Title. II. Series.
   SB327.S65 2005
   635'.652--dc22

                                        2004020249

Acknowledgments
The author and publisher are grateful to the following for permission to reproduce copyright material: Anthony Blake p. 22; Chris Honeywell p. 17; Corbis pp. 5 (Michael Boys), 7 (Robert Maass); Garden Picture Library pp. 13 (Howard Rice), 19 (Steven Wooster); Holt Studios pp. 12 (Nigel Cattlin), 18 (Inga Spence), 23 (pod, Inga Spence); Nature Picture Library pp. 15 (John B. Free), 16 (Premaphotos), 23 (nectar, John B. Free; pollen, Premaphotos); Oxford Scientific Films pp. 6, 8, 9, 10, 11, 23 (root, seed, shoot), back cover; Photo Horticultural pp. 4 (Michael & Lois Warren), 14; The Garden Picture pp. 20, 21 (David Askham)

Cover photograph of beans reproduced with permission of FLPA (Richard Becker)

Every effort has been made to contact copyright holders of any material reproduced in this book. Any omissions will be rectified in subsequent printings if notice is given to the publisher.

Many thanks to the teachers, library media specialists, reading instructors, and educational consultants who have helped develop the Read and Learn/Lee y aprende brand.

Contents

Some words are shown in bold, **like this.** You can find them in the picture glossary on page 23.

What Is a Bean?

Beans are a kind of **seed**.

They grow inside a **pod**.

We can cook beans and
eat them.

Where Do Beans Grow?

A bean plant starts life as a bean **seed**.

People put bean seeds in dirt.

The seeds need water to help them grow into plants.

More beans grow on the plants.

How Do Bean Plants Grow?

First, a **root** grows.

It grows out of the **seed** and down into the dirt.

Next, a **stem** starts to grow.

The stem grows up.

What Do Roots and Stems Do?

The **stem** grows up out of the dirt.

It grows towards the light.

The **root** grows lots of little roots.

They take up water and food for the plant.

What Else Grows On Bean Plants?

After about 3 weeks, leaves begin to grow on the bean plant.

The leaves are dark green.

A few weeks later, flowers start
to grow.

What Do the Flowers Do?

The flowers on the bean plants make **pollen.**

Pollen is a yellow dust inside the flowers.

Bees drink a sweet juice called **nectar** from inside the flowers.

The pollen rubs onto the bees.

How Do Bees Help Beans Grow?

Bees help beans grow.

Pollen from the flower sticks to the bees.

Bees fly to different flowers and
take the pollen to them.

The pollen helps to start a bean
growing in the flower.

How Do Beans Grow?

The flowers die and drop off the plants.

The beans grow inside **pods**.

The pods keep the beans safe.

Inside the pods it is soft and damp.

When Are Beans Ready to Eat?

In summer, the beans and pods are big and long.

It is time to pick and eat the beans.

In fall, the bean plant turns brown and dies.

You can use the brown beans to grow new plants.

Bean Diagram

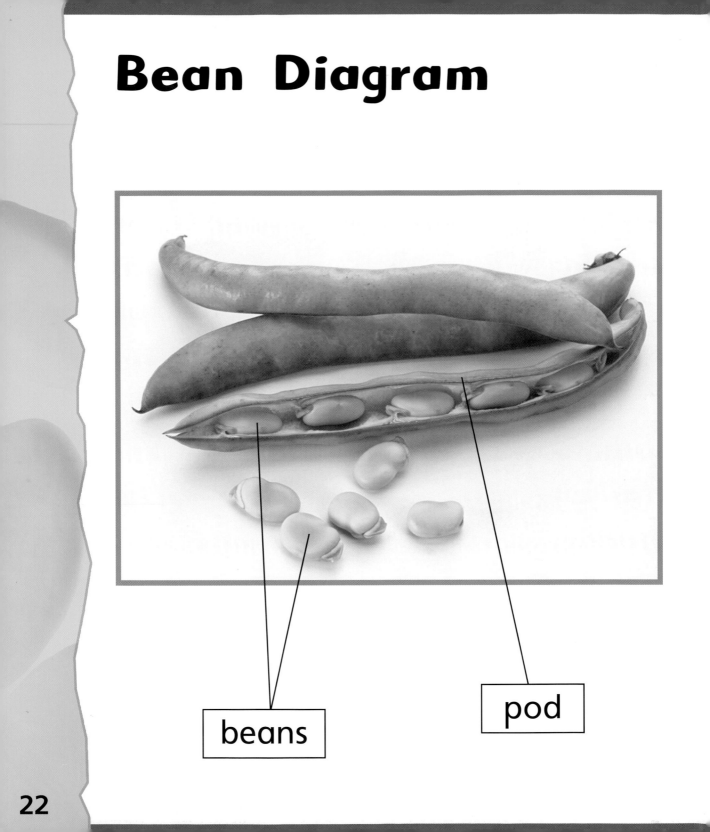

beans

pod

Picture Glossary

nectar
page 15
sweet juice in the center of a flower

pod
page 4
part of a plant where beans grow

pollen
pages 14, 15, 16, 17
yellow dust in flowers

root
pages 8, 11
part of a plant that grows under the ground. It takes in water for a plant.

seed
pages 4, 6, 8
beans are a kind of seed. Plants grow from seeds.

stem
pages 9, 10
first part of the plant that grows out of the ground. It takes in light for a plant.

Note to Parents and Teachers

Reading for information is an important part of a child's literacy development. Learning begins with a question about something. Help children think of themselves as investigators and researchers by encouraging their questions about the world around them. Each chapter in this book begins with a question. Read the question together. Look at the pictures. Talk about what you think the answer might be. Then read the text to find out if your predictions were correct. Think of other questions you could ask about the topic, and discuss where you might find the answers. Assist children in using the picture glossary and the index to practice new vocabulary and research skills.

Index